Film For Her

A Book for Women

Rishiba S

ISBN 978-93-5610-805-9

Published in India 2022 by Pencil

A brand of
One Point Six Technologies Pvt. Ltd.
123, Building J2, Shram Seva Premises,
Wadala Truck Terminal, Wadala (E)
Mumbai 400037, Maharashtra, INDIA
E connect@thepencilapp.com
W www.thepencilapp.com

DISCLAIMER: *The opinions expressed in this book are those of the authors and do not purport to reflect the views of the Publisher.*

Author biography

Rishiba S is 20 years old college student and an aspiring poet. She was born on 06 June 2002 at Kerala. She is the eldest daughter of Mr. Sasi Kumar K and Mrs. Jasmine S. She is pursuing bachelors of English literature at Mahatma Gandhi University, Kerala. Rishiba has taken a keen interest in writing and has been an avid reader her whole life. Her days were spent reading and putting her thoughts into words. As much as she loves reading and writing, the same will always be her passion. Writing is the thing that she finds more solace in. She had a special anthology for one of her poem titled "Cry of a Woman". What lies within is, Rishiba's first book, it's a collection of poems that will reach your heart and stir your soul. With this book, the author wants to take you on an emotional journey of being a woman.

CONTENTS

Epigraph

Tremendous amounts of talent are being lost to our society just because that talent wears a skirt.

- Shirley Chisholm

Preface

The age of a woman doesn't mean a thing. The best times are played on the oldest fiddles."

- Ralph Waldo Emerson

"Film for Her" is a poetry collection portraying the journey of being a woman. I put across an ocean, a world, and a galaxy; I altered for you to read and realize that women are not alone in her battles. These are my words, and my heart laid bare, for you to see, read and understand that everyone fights a million battles, but not everyone can equal a woman. These are poems about the different stages of women and the struggles she faces in her life. It is also about how she plant a seed of hope, and she waits and wait as if it would never grow, but it grows and enters her life, like that morning light enters the room through the blinds, subtle and soft, yet making everything glow in its wake. I hope that readers of this book will be inspired and motivated through my lines.

Acknowledgements

I stared at the blank page for a whole of 30 minutes before starting to write this acknowledgement. There is just so much to say, so much to be grateful for, so many people to thank. First things first, this is for my parents, family, and my friends, all of you are my backbone, my spine, and my entire being would collapse without you all.

To my parents, how do I even thank you both for everything you have ever done for me, it's quite literally impossible. I have absolutely no idea where to begin and where to end, a simple thank you wouldn't suffice. But that's all I have got, so thank you for being the best parents out there,, and thank you for supporting my extremely ambitious dreams.

To my sister, I thank you for reading every unedited, full of mistake pieces I ever wrote. You complained a little and whined a little, but in the end were always there. Thank you for understanding my typos and errors. Thank you for everything.

To my family, you gave me the gentle push when I needed it and words of encouragement when I was down. A lifetime isn't enough to hold the amount of gratitude I have for you, and it's your undying support and love that I am here, no words are enough to thank you.

To my friends, thank you for always reading what I wrote, even the most trivial and mundane things. I couldn't be more grateful to have you in my life. Thank you for existing and tolerating my annoying self,, and thank you for always being there.

Finally, I would like to thank everyone from the Pencil team who made this book come true. If it weren't you all, this book would have just remained a dream. I would like to thank everyone else who were involved in the different processes of making this book reach shelves.

Dedication

This book is dedicated to all the women.

Women are the epitome of wealth and power. Women play an important role in society, and the whole family is dependent on women for its daily activities. They play the role of mother, wife, homemaker, cook, teacher, friend, nurse all at the same time while catering to everybody's needs. The life of women is very hard, but she gets little or no appreciation. One of the major hindrances in the growth and advancement of women is gender inequality. As divorce is still a taboo in Indian society, many women are suffering from abusive marriages. The women hardly get economic independence. If we wish to see a nation that develops economically on the global front, then it's vital to have "Women Empowerment". The true meaning of women empowerment will be achieved when gender inequality will be to eliminate. We look forward to such a nation.

Death Before Birth

It is dark here, mama,
I feel frightened and alone.
My tiny little fingers,
Seem impatient to clasp yours.
The little heart, within me,
Pounds excitedly as the day nears.
Oh, I just can't wait,
To live this beautiful life you are gifting me.
I fail to express my gratitude,
To you, for creating me.
I sleep, I eat, I kick, and I play,
I hear your sweet voice throughout the day,
Immense joy and no sorrow to hide.
I spend my time hearing you sing,
Songs of happiness, songs of spring.
I sensed your hurt last night when you cried
I sense tears in your eyes,
Is there something amiss, mama?

Your hurt and vibrations make me nervous,
Your cry and emotions make me anxious.
I whispered, I kicked, but you never replied,
I am scared, I am confused,
What's all the turmoil?
Mama replied,
Shh, they want a boy and not a girl,
Boy is treated as diamond and pearl.
I feel sorry, your life is short inside,
The world is sick and unsafe outside.
Oh mother, save me, what have I done wrong?
Am I not dear to you? Am I not worth your time?
Is being a girl in this world my only crime?
Don't I even deserve your love, hug, or a kiss?
You don't want me to play, jump and run,
All you want for yourself is a son!
The wails, the shout, the cries,
It feels as if it's being heard by deaf ears.
I am just a baby not yet developed,
Give me a chance, I'll rise to your expectations.

So what? If I am not a boy, I'll be your girl,
I'll be your support, I'll be your joy.
I promise! I shall.
No! Please don't abandon me,
I am your part, don't kill me.
Why do they detest me so much?
Just because I am a girl?
Please don't nip me in the bud,
I was planned this way,
How am I to be blamed?
The smothering hatred outside,
Feels darker than the darkness here.
That seems like an old lost dream,
And I can't scream,
For I have got no say,
Perhaps my life will end in such a way.
I am struck inside,
And have no power to decide.
My dreams and life are lost,
As she's finally decided to abort.

Hush, Baby Girl

When she was born,
There was no celebration,
Even there was a negative situation.
It was too hard for her to born,
Society was too prone,
Prone of the female child born.
She was born among shouts and cries,
Had it been a boy,
They would have smiled,
But they did mourn,
For as a girl, she was born.
She looked so cute and kind,
But no happiness did the parents find.
They don't love her,
They don't even care,
At the same time pampering her brother.
They thought she was a fool and despised her,
Isn't it unfair?

She doesn't know what's going on,
She was taught to stay at home,
Doing all the household chores alone.
She was taught not to decide on her own,
Accept the things and move on,
Move on from the freedom of her mind.
She was a precious gift of god,
But they did not send her to school.
She needed love and care,
But people around make her life a scare.
They pushed her around,
Made her sleep on the ground.
When things go wrong,
She was taught to bear the pain.
How much violence she has to abide,
From harassment to being burned,
She has to accept everything and learn.

She knows life is a game,
And she was a good player.
She was ready to accept,
Each and every dare.
She was hopeful that,
She will be successful someday.
She will achieve her goal,
It might be difficult, but she'll find a way.
She was practicing a lot,
Each day and every day.
She always thinks what was her fault,
If she was a girl child born.
She never got the answer,
Until her death comes alive.
She took her last breath and cried,
" Never make me a girl again
Because I can't bear this pain again".

The Hidden Star

At 14 while on her first period,
Not aware of the deadly pain.
Red drops on the floor,
They were laughing- "it's so sad".
No one saw that blooded body,
As they pass nearby.
But they noticed those,
Small blood stain on her skirt.
On a red dot on her white dress,
She searches for her mother.
Held the stomach and fell on bed,
Said to mom, "I am dying".
Mom hold her on arms,
"My girl you are growing not bad".
Not clear, still confused on blood,
Why pain on stomach.
Sight from society, fun they made,
Sad during the pain and can't share.

On those five days every month,
Happy times fails.
Then rain showers of pain,
And merry became wails.
It is that time of the month,
When happy games shut,
For the angels knife cut,
And dirty rivers flow.
Feeling intestines entangle,
In the abdomen beneath.
Contracting every muscle,
And for so long, gnawing the teeth.
Impure and Unholy,
She bleeds,
She is unsafe and untouchable,
Her menstrual blood is impure,
The society labels her unabashedly.
Why carry pads in black polythene bags?
Why to tell it in ears?
Why? She asks.

Oh, darling girl,
Your period isn't dirty.
It is the same blood,
That holds them for,
So long, nine months.
Your period is the ocean tide,
That smooths the sand,
And rises with the moon.
It is a glacial waterfall,
That freezes in the winter,
And flows in the summer.
Out of the greatest passage,
As new ovaries develop,
Making fertile the virgin lands,
And yet another may come,
You will find your path over time.
Isn't it a matter of great pride?
And one day I hope you'll think,
Today I am bleeding,
Today I am healthy,
Today I am alive.

Just Listen

A father asks his daughter,
Study? Why should you study?
I have sons who can study,
Girl, why should you study?
The daughter tells her father,
Why can't I study?
I am not just born to make tea.
I must study,
To fight my battles,
To bring new light to my knowledge,
And to avoid destitution.
My heart pains badly,
When I say this sadly.
You don't know how I feel,
When children carry bags and meal.
Just listen! Just listen!
Because I am a girl, I must study.

I am just a small child,
Who is so gentle and mild.
I must study,
To fight frustration and find inspiration,
To challenge patriarchy,
And to demolish all hierarchy.
Let me go to school,
For I would rather not be a fool.
I must study,
To know right from wrong,
To sweep centuries of dust,
And to challenge what I must.
To find a strong voice,
And to make a world where girls belong,
I must study.
Just listen! Just listen!
Because I am a girl, I must study.

Just listen! Just listen!
What a girl child says,
Why can't I study?
Education meant much to me,
It's the right since birth,
Which can't be abided.
Why not I be the one,
Being taught in the school?
Oh father, just give me one chance,
Then before you, I will glow like a pearl,
And I will be at glance.
Just listen! Just listen!
Because I am a girl, I must study.
Let me study! Let me enjoy!

An Evil Act

It began as a typical Sunday,
Sunlight kissed her eyelids.
She decorated herself,
Like the walls of her home.
She hung a necklace around her neck,
Hooked earrings in,
Applied lipstick like paint,
And swept her hair back.
It's just a typical Sunday,
It ended up at a get-together with friends,
He asked if she needed a ride home,
She said yes cause he's her friend.
But she should have known,
When he began to confuse.
There was a change in him,
His words and actions were violent,
He was drunk,
She was scared and left.

Film For Her

She sat alone in the cold, dark room,
She heard a car park outside.
The door opened viciously,
She would run for it if she could.
He dragged her out of the bed,
Kicked her and punched her.
Cowering in fright, she began to plea,
"Please, don't do this to me".
But it was already too late,
The alcohol decided her fate.
She got his fingerprints all over her body,
Her deep inside horrendous screams,
He tortured and kills her nature.
She cried out of her heart,
And suffered a never-ending pain.
She really wished people knew,
Of the pain she goes through.
She dreamt a world where she was free,
But it was just a dream.

Film For Her

A pill to numb her pain,
Makeup to cover her scars,
Shirts with long sleeves,
And bandages on her arms,
She kept quite hoping it will stop.
One day, when he gets sober,
And reason takes over,
She phoned the police,
But they just made a report,
And said, she will be fine.
He got mad and stripped her naked,
Beat her with a plank.
She couldn't take it anymore,
Took a kitchen knife,
And stabbed the drunk man.
But, will it erase her dirty chapter?
Or, can anyone return her purity?
As she grows from nineteen to ninety,
The bitter truth will stand before her,
And she will know of true shame.
Will she ever stop telling,
"I was raped at my nineteen,
And lost my innocence and life"

Her Parity

Gender equality,
What we have been seeking for,
Agreed with it.
In today's world,
Women are allowed to be part of working,
And they can go on with pants and shirts.
Yet, I disagree,
When she had the capability,
She manages things well solely.
But when it comes to decision-making at home,
A sound rings hard in her ears,
"I'm the man of the house,
And I'm the decision maker".
In a flash,
Gender equality lost identity.
Why can't she be heard too?
Where did the society go from,
One for all and all for one?

She is a daughter, sister and mother,
Then why always she suffers?
Why do we differentiate between him and she?
God didn't, then why do we?
Equality doesn't discriminate,
The rights of the women and men.
Being born as a girl,
There is need to educate.
And not a boy,
Does not make you inadequate.
Being queer is natural,
It's not a joke or illness.
Accept, don't differentiate,
Let her race wearing her spikes,
Or lead in her heels in a corporate.
She can choose to marry or not,
Or celebrate her individuality.

He and she, they both have quality,
So prefer gender equality.
Recognise innate talent,
Why stare at her assets.
Equal pay, for equal efforts,
Should be a basic mandate.
Time to embrace and liberate,
Aren't we all?
Just as queer as we are straight?
Ditch the binary, adapt the plural,
Let's give our gender norms an update.
We won't yield,
So don't dominate.
We are unified against oppression,
And won't let you manipulate.
We have one aim,
Patriarchy, soon you shall disintegrate.

Her Silent Whisper

She whispers in a silent room
I'm the woman I can be,
And I have my side of vulnerability,
I live and deal with them,
I have that capability,
I'm not here to be taken for a ride,
And not here for your sexual drive.
I'm a woman with strength,
I have seen the worst and still stand,
I smile through those difficult times,
I believe in myself, the power in my hand,
I'm not here for you to abuse,
And not here for you to use.
Help me, hear my cries,
I'm a diamond, a jewel,
Why are you so cruel?
I'm a woman and I deserve more.

I whisper with my torn heart
I'm a woman of thoughts,
I pen them down as they are,
The lines I write reflect my image,
They can even show my inner war,
I'm not here for you to hurt me,
And not here for you to kill me.
I'm a woman who believes,
Love, hope and humanity still exists,
Jealousy and hatred has no place in me,
It is something my mind resists,
I'm not here to be your side fling,
And not here for you to make me sing.
Beating, beating and beating me,
Is like you want me to go insane,
Is this what I am really here for?
I'm a woman and I deserve more.

I'm a woman of substance,
And I know my worth,
I hold my dignity and respect,
I'm here to hold my place on mother earth,
I'm not here for you,
To tell me your bitter lies,
And I'm not here for you,
To squeeze my heart until it breaks.
With pain until I'm pulling my hair,
And you just don't care,
I'm crying, I'm crying tears of blood,
I'm dying inside,
My heart is going to the pearly gates,
Last tear of blood rolls down,
I'm a woman and I deserve more.

No, It Ain't Fair

Forced into a situation,
That she didn't choose.
Not old enough,
To lighten up with booze.
She didn't know the man,
She didn't want to marry.
They called him,
To build her world.
It's truly an atrocious thing,
Only disasters it will bring.
She is not yet mentally prepared,
To face the marriage life.
The first time she met him,
A flash forward of her life, what a fright.
It's a scheme, a marketing ploy,
That family pressures on her.
As they continue the holy procession,
She cried with her ripped heart.

She says,
I had rather been all by myself,
Than to marry a man for wealth.
Young, wild and free,
I swear that's how it should be.
No being forced into things,
I want to fly away,
Where are my wings?
Mom, Dad, don't you love me?
I'm still so young,
Let me just be.
Mom, Dad, can't you see?
It's wrong to marry a man for his wealth.
Best days of a girl's life,
That's what they say,
Surely not marrying this way.
And please let me just say,
No other should endure her life this way.

Mama,
What have I done to deserve this?
Why force someone on my neck?
Why bring someone that I hated?
Why bring someone that my heart knows not?
Oh father,
I'm not of age now,
I know what is good for me,
I may have delayed bringing your in laws,
But forcing him on me is shameful.
Tell me it is not true,
And you were kidding.
Tell me you didn't mean your words,
That you had found a man for me.
They replied,
We have made up our mind,
And she was forced to bear it forever.

They Demands

Perfectly imperfect at the beginning,
Groom asked for a gold,
And demanded money and more,
A car, a new phone and ten lakh.
Her father says,
For I owe a female child,
I'll leave thee then completely rich.
My daughter's dowry, having which,
Gold, pearl, rubies, bonds,
Long forfeits, pawned diamonds,
And antique pledges, house or land.
But it wasn't enough for him,
He considered her unworthy,
And she's no value to him.
He says, "To take her off your hands,
I need a car and ten lakh too".
Her parents cried,
For they can't buy a car.

Seeing her parents suffer,
She stood up and speaks,
Bride is a dowry,
Why does groom want gold?
Keep your tongue on hold,
And stop asking my price,
For only the bride is a dowry.
She is not a commodity of trading,
And her life shall not be weighed.
Wedding is for two loving hearts,
Not for others 'Game of Cowry'.
Money can't be the solution of strife,
Being gentle is enough for her.
Any property, for the marriage,
Calls for modern enslavement.
Giving gifts will sound a solution,
Or we say bride price is an option,
But we can't make marriage an auction.

Film For Her

A burden for her parents,
Yet they're paying the price.
She sits in place of her doll,
Beside her is husband-to-be,
With gold, money and more.
And her fate?
Broken as sharp pieces of glass.
In the name of marriage,
She was sold forever.
Those people are very self-seeking,
Who calls dowry as love greeting.
They don't even feels embarrassed,
And asks her father did they, harassed.
He was too quite during their marriage,
Who is well known as her husband.
After two mornings, he tormented her,
Yelled at her to give more land.
No one offend, so through marriage,
Dowry they claim.

The Blessed Curse

A little bird trapped in a cage,
Marrying a man for his wage.
Trapped forever silently,
In sickness and in health.
She was so happy,
Is what to say, in denial.
No control of her life,
Walking down the aisle.
She's someone's possession,
It's At this moment,
She didn't want to die.
But it doesn't mean,
She wants to be alive.
Rough face covered with make up,
Thought she was loved,
But ended up being lusted for.
Any decision made by her,
Was thrashed for it.

She loved her marriage,
Yet in bondage.
The beautiful face she had,
Has been scraped off now.
She was forced to live with him,
Even he beats her.
Thought it's compromise,
Didn't know it's authorized.
If she does or say the right thing,
She's being questioned for it.
Daylight is like darkness,
While every night is like,
"I'm pinned in the heart".
The scars are so scary,
Thought there will be a change,
But ended up being a challenge.
A marriage full of pretence,
She's made to be silent.

Circumstances getting out of hand,
From love rain to violence.
Forced to tell the world it's alright,
When it's never fine.
Her husband beats every day,
She cries in pain,
But no one cares and say's 'don't cry'.
Only she hears how bad she was,
It hurts, she feels she didn't deserve to live.
She has to obey everyone's orders,
However bad they are.
Just few hours of sleep at night,
Bruises, and pains in body,
She hid all this from her parents.
She likes to run away, but where will she go?
She didn't have a house of own.
She lived a life of living dead,
And, hence, a blessed curse.

Aching Heart

Aching heart, empty arms,
Spinning in dizzying circles for eternity.
A dream she had for so long,
To carry something inside her,
A childless woman she was.
Rapt in her white shawl,
She's out in the storm,
Crying for a baby.
A childless woman, drenched to the bone,
Walks around endlessly weeping alone.
Goes to doctor year after year,
Just to hear everything is normal.
She wants to know what's stopping her,
What's holding back from her dreams.
Sporadically she had been so remarkable,
And occasionally she craves each day.
Every month was too hard,
And she feels each year a ticking bomb.

The childless woman prays every day,
That a child will come her way.
She had a couple of options left,
Either a surrogate mother or to adopt.
She spoke with her family,
But the answer is "No".
Society labels her unholy,
She tried to keep her head high,
Hoping for the best,
Yet fighting the question, why.
Withering away, slowly dying,
Swollen eyes from all the crying.
Pounding heart, soaring fears, fragile soul,
The hurt, and pains continues to grow.
Praying and pleading to god,
Begging god to hear her prayers.
She cried, "I want to be a mother,
I need to be".

A childless woman is rocking herself to sleep,
Dreaming, one day,
She'll stroll with pram across the street,
With a baby of her own.
Gazing up to the goodness,
Which looks down from the skies.
A childless woman now,
She's only got a short grip on life,
Wants to be a good mother.
A childless woman now,
Her only one wish, to command,
A crying little infant.
Rapt in a shawl, oh,
He's so tender and meek,
He has got ten little fingers.
Her mind is twisting out of control,
She cries,
I need help, I need healing.

Pregnant Pause

A man is so glad to know,
That inside her, his child grows.
As her stomach starts to grow,
Her soft caressing hands begin to show,
And her face take on a radiant glow.
She sees her life in a different way,
As her motherly instincts come into play.
Those nine months of sleepless nights,
Had not driven her insane.
She says,
Running errands and talking on the phone,
I'm pleasantly remained that I'm not alone.
Little tiny hands, a precious rounded knee,
Pushing and twisting that no one can see.
Oh sweet child, kicking up your heels,
It is our little secret that only I can feel.
I look forward to your birth,
As I feel you play within.

Her little unborn whispers,
Mummy, can you feel me?
I'm wriggling for you.
I can hear you say you love me,
Mum, I love you too.
Very soon, you'll meet me,
And kiss my little face.
Mummy, are you ready?
My life is just about to start.
She was sick, sick in her body,
Eyes wide open, silent,
She lay on the bed of childbirth.
There was pain, blood and screaming,
And uncontrollably tremble with dread.
She was all alone,
Totally, utterly, entirely on her own.
Gnawing her lips, holding her body rigid,
Waiting on inexorable fate.

The wind blows the pollen at night,
Through ruins of fields and homes.
Earth shivers with love,
With the pain of giving birth.
The scarred land inaugurates life,
As the rose of blood blooms on the wound.
The beating of its mother's heart,
Had become as one,
And a new life had begun.
The sight of something, so beautiful,
Made her forget all the pain.
She feels like God for a moment,
To have created a life.
Out of her flesh and blood,
Was made her darling child.
She had become what God intended,
A mother of life-of hopes and dreams.

Your Mother's Perfume

A state of selflessness,
The home of true love,
The soul that lives for others,
And a place where compassion lives.
The pillar of every home,
The watch of heritage,
The birth of Empire,
And the spring of being.
The definition of sacrifice,
And the sanctuary of trust.
The hand that takes all blames,
For wrongs she knows nothing about.
Selfishness had no place in her,
And takes the last dish at every meal.
Countless sleepless nights,
Yet working without a beat.
Who was she?
She was an angel-Mother.

For nine months she bore the pain,
Expecting nothing but a mother's gain.
That deadly labor pain,
Now become a perfect seed.
She's more than a woman,
She is a mother indeed.
Denying herself luxuries,
She provided all your needs.
She gave you a name befitting her beliefs,
And you designed her clothes with infancy stains.
She is like a mother hen,
Shivering under a thunderous rain,
And covering the chicks with her soaked wings.
True love and gentleness can be felt,
As she walks through your life.
She was always there to give a hug,
And tries to make you smile.
She holds you in her heart,
When you are filled with all fears.

Mothers heal cuts and bruises,
Shelter children from each storm.
Supports you through all thick and thin,
And provides hugs that feel safe and warm.
There's nothing better than mother's love,
She was the one who dearly loves,
And is always there,
From scraped knees to falls from trees.
She had become a mentor and a guide,
Within her always you would confide.
No better payment for her could be found,
Than to love her with heart.
A mother's love endures forever,
It is patient and forgiving.
When all others are forsaking,
It never fails or falters.
She is another wondrous evidence,
Of God's tender guiding hands.

On a Tired Housewife

They call her "Just a housewife",
And she was glad to bear the name.
You will never see her listed,
On the "Honor roll of fame".
As she washes the floors and windows,
Stylish women pity her.
She works hard at trying,
To be a more considerable wife.
She was the keeper of a household,
Which is "Home sweet home".
She was rich in love,
And work hard in her old life.
Career women look, with pity,
At her apron, broom and mop.
But she wouldn't trade them places,
For the things their money brought.
Yes, they call her "Just a housewife",
But she's more-much more, they see.

She rises at break of day,
And through her tasks she races.
Cooks the meal as best she may,
And bakes pudding.
Cleans the rooms up one by one,
With one eye watching her baby.
The mending pile she then attacks,
By way of variation.
She irons a little while,
Then presses pants for daddy.
She welcomes with a smile,
Returning lass and laddie.
A hearty dinner next she cooks,
No time for relaxation.
While schoolbooks, lunches, and ribbons,
All need consideration.
And yet, the census man insists,
She has "No occupation".

She cries,
I bend and rise with the grace,
And smash cloves.
Repeat a kitchen experiment,
And I'm spent on the oven.
I find myself in pin and needle,
In buckled patterns.
Sweeping, dusting and mopping,
Always moving and never stopping.
Then trying to look pretty,
When my husband gets home.
See, I am cumbered,
With serving and with small vexatious things.
Upstairs and down my feet,
So tired, I cannot mount up with wings.
At last, I laid aside,
With leisured feet and idle hands.
And with my heart's door open,
Ends the housewife's day.

Breaking Free

Marriage sacred and sanctified,
Why divorce?
Who divorced who?
They became attached to one another,
Commit to stay together,
And mingle as a life partner.
Days and weeks passes,
Family grows but,
Bonds of love they share,
Seems to be declining.
Arguments and blame game begins,
Trust and hope fades.
Commitment they made,
Were only on lips.
Her heart wounded and pierced,
Cursed and caused to weep.
But she forgives, and
Bears the sweet pain.

She treasures and pleasures him,
But he acquired her friend's hip.
Her heart heaps and worries,
And her knees humble in prayers.
Her love clings to him in matrimony,
Why bull and battle her?
Rumours roared in the air,
Heard but never caught.
He filed a divorce,
She pleads his deaf ears,
Ignorantly he ignores her.
He leaves her and kids behind,
Before the death knell paper was signed.
Everything got dark,
And their relationship went straight to abyss,
They were officially separated.
She felt lost, rejected and defeated,
While he seemed happy.

They advised her,
Your husband left you two years ago,
And you've been waiting for him.
You thought he was going to come back,
But he deceived you and committed bigamy.
Another woman took him,
That makes the emotional pain hurt deeper.
He married a woman,
And I saw her picture in a social media.
If you had the chance,
You had probably taken him back,
For still, you love him.
But that's impossible,
You should be practical,
And it's time to give up.
She replied with teary eyes,
We are apart,
I just pray that we can find peace.
We are now split,
Separated forever for eternity.

Being Aged

As a white candle in a holy place,
So is the beauty of her aged face.
As the spent radiance of the winter sun,
So is the woman with her travail done.
Thousands of wrinkles on her forehead,
Depicting worries and agony.
Left isolated in huge brick walls,
Cursing the rough luck that have fall upon.
As she rummages through the pages of her life,
She remembers her married life,
The hustle, the joys, and the strife.
She was the mother of three children,
It was not easy,
Taking care of their studies,
And getting them married.
They moved to another house,
Life got busier,
And she had to take care of her grand children.

Now she was bedridden,
They have put her in an old age home.
Maid takes care of everything,
She merely sits and think,
"Why I sacrificed my youth and savings,
On these selfish beings.
I wish I had enjoyed life,
Instead of serving them day and night".
They treated her like a piece of wood,
Chucked her out when she was of no use.
She didn't want material comforts,
But love and joyful faces.
She searches for people with feelings,
And longs to hear, "I care for your well-being".
Children rarely visit her,
That was awful indeed and painful.
Even the bare walls laugh at her,
For all her stupidity.

She longs to talk to someone,
They need not be her own.
The maid does her duty,
Finishes fast and goes away.
She has no love for the old aged woman,
But she wishes at least she would stay.
Life of love and compassion,
Different festivals in different seasons,
She lives them in her imaginary world.
Always thinking about her death,
She had three sons to lit her funeral pyre,
But now that confidence is no longer there.
Isolated, secluded and forlorn,
She rests in an old age home.
Eyes always at door and phone,
Waiting for their visit or a call.
Disappointment every day beguiled,
Heart shattered and eyes turned into stone,
Blind faith still recreating a hope.

A Woman Speaks

It is hard to be a woman,
Yes, it's difficult to enter this world.
Murdering her in the womb,
Was called a treason.
Taking birth into this world,
Is no less than a prison.
Fed up with dowry,
And fed up with harassment.
She wanted to get vanish away,
From this race.
That girl,
Has fought a thousand battles,
Has cried a million tears,
And has been broken,
Betrayed, abandoned and rejected.
Yet, being the purest form of a happy spirit,
She makes her way,
And lights up a room.

They tried to cage and contain her,
Drain her of her worth.
Beat her down to nothing,
With relentless fists or words.
Control and de-soul her,
But she is resilient.
Now taking back her true form,
Beautiful yet so strong,
Independent yet so elegant,
Young yet so intelligent,
Kind yet so aggressive.
Full of hopes, full of dreams,
And full of enthusiasm, never mean.
Took the challenges with a bang,
Never staying with the same old things.
Always smiling and impressive,
She had dreams, ambition
And she had morals.

Their hungry night tried to devour her,
But she made her own light,
That darkness could not swallow.
She has carried life, hidden within,
A seedling growing skyward.
Took everything like a component,
Fighting with a straight face.
They set out to mess with her,
But she had beat them,
Not with fists but with words.
Oppressed no longer,
She sought to make her mark,
And stood up like a storm in this greedy world.
She is no lesser than any man,
She is the warrior of life,
Not a complicated mother, daughter, or a wife.
Filled with a vision, she will walk,
Empowering those for her gender.
She will rise,
She will shine,
She will,
Unstoppable.

Glossary

Amiss: wrong
Turmoil: a state of great noise or confusion
Abandon: to leave somebody or something
Nip: to give somebody or something a quick bite or to quickly squeeze a piece of somebody's skin between your thumb and finger.
Smothering: to kill somebody by covering his or her face so that he or she cannot breathe.
Prone: likely to suffer from something or to do something bad
Mourn: to feel and show great sadness, especially because somebody has died
Pampering: to take care of somebody very well and make him or her feel as comfortable as possible.
Despised: to hate somebody or something very much
Abide: accept or act in accordance with
Entangle: cause to become twisted together with or caught in
Gnawing: to bite a bone, etc. many times with your back teeth
Unabashedly: without embarrassment or shame
Destitution: poverty so extreme that one lacks the means to provide for oneself
Demolish: to destroy something
Viciously: in a cruel or violent manner

Cowering: to move back or into a low position because of fear
Horrendous: very bad or unpleasant
Sober: serious
Plank: a long flat thin piece of wood that is used for building or making things

Queer: strange or unusual
Innate: used about an ability or a quality that you have when you are born
Atrocious: extremely bad or unpleasant
Ploy: something that you say or do in order to get what you want or to persuade somebody to do something
Strife: trouble or fighting between people or groups
Auction: a public sale at which items are sold to the person who offers to pay the most money
Tormented: experiencing or characterized by severe physical or mental suffering
Aisle: a passage between the rows of seats in a church, theatre, etc
Bondage: the state of being a slave
Pretence: an action that makes people believe something that is not true
Bruises: a blue, brown or purple mark that appears on the skin after somebody has fallen, been hit, etc
Dizzying: causing someone to feel unsteady, confused, or amazed
Rapt: so interested in one particular thing that you do not notice anything else
Drenched: to make somebody or something completely wet
Withering: done to make somebody feel silly or embarrassed
Fragile: easily damaged or broken
Stroll: a slow walk for pleasure
Pram: a small vehicle on four wheels for a baby, pushed by a person on foot
Caressing: to touch somebody or something in a gentle and loving way

Errands: a short journey to take or get something for somebody

Wriggling: to move about, or to move a part of your body, with short, quick movements, especially from side to side
Tremble: to shake, for example because you are cold, frightened, etc
Dread: to be very afraid of or worried about something
Inexorable: impossible to stop or prevent
Befitting: appropriate to the occasion
Confide: to tell somebody something that is secret
Pity: a feeling of sadness that you have for somebody or something that is suffering or in trouble
Lass: a girl or young woman
Cumbered: hamper or hinder
Sanctified: set apart as or declare holy; consecrate
Abyss: a very deep hole that seems to have no bottom
Deceived: to try to make somebody believe something that is not true
Bigamy: the state of being married to two people at the same time
Travail: painful or laborious effort
Rummage: to move things
Chucked: to throw something in a careless way
Pyre: a large pile of wood on which a dead body is placed and burned as part of a funeral ceremony
Forlorn: lonely and unhappy; not cared for
Beguiled: deceive, mislead
Treason: the criminal act of causing harm to your country
Fist: a hand with the fingers closed together tightly

Bibliography

https://mymodernmet.com/inspirational-quotes-women/

www.ingramcontent.com/pod-product-compliance
Lightning Source LLC
LaVergne TN
LVHW050421160726
843469LV00041B/1180